PUTTING ME BACK TOGETHER

Lynn Mintz

ISBN 979-8-88832-945-0 (paperback)
ISBN 979-8-88832-946-7 (digital)

Christian Faith Publishing
832 Park Avenue
Meadville, PA 16335
www.christianfaithpublishing.com

Printed in the United States of America

ACKNOWLEDGMENTS

To my children. I love you, guys, very much. I have always been honored to have you as my children. I wish I could go back to when you, guys, were little and undo so much. I can't though, and all I can do is ask for your forgiveness. I pray and know that God will restore my family! I know you, guys, have gone through your own pain. I ask that you cry out to the only one that can heal and fix anything. I love you and want the best for both of you. But most of all, I want you free from pain. I am so sorry for failing you. You, guys, are the world to me. I will never stop loving you and praying for you.

Love,
Mom

To my beautiful granddaughters. Trust, Grandma, when I say never try to do this world without God. For he is the only true answer to peace and healing. I love you and will never stop praying for you. To my oldest granddaughter, I have watched you grow into a wonderful young lady of God. Never stop trusting him. I'm so excited to see what he has in store for you. To my youngest one, as our relationship grows, my prayer for you is that you will find out how awesome God truly is. And that he will become a big part of your life. I love you both very much.

Love,
Grandma

INTRODUCTION

I am a woman who has gone through a lot of abuse. Believe me when I say it would be easy to keep this to myself, but if I can help just one person, it will be worth it. God has changed me, healed me, and he is still doing a work in me. The only difference is I'm open to the change. I am so in love with Jesus that I would be so wrong not to tell my story about how wonderful he is and how he saved me. I honestly hope this book helps many. I have kept things exceptionally clean cut; I don't feel the need to get into graphic details. That is not the point of the book. The point is that no matter how low or far we feel we have gone, God will never leave us. He loves us *no matter* what. Thank you for taking the time to hear my testimony. God bless!

CHAPTER 1

Silent Cry

Hello, my name is Lynn, and I would consider myself a very blessed woman today. Many may look at my life and may not feel the same way, or maybe feel it is overstated, but if you knew where I came from, you might agree with me.

I grew up in Chicago, and I was an only child. My mother miscarried twin girls at six months. In a way, I felt that was a good thing, or they could have been victims as well. I do often wonder if I had my sisters, would it have changed things at all? Or would we all have to deal with the things my father did? It was hard being alone. I had no one to turn to that I trusted. After any incident, I would play outside by myself. I had no one. I was a tomboy because there were mainly boys in the neighborhood. I learned how to climb trees and would climb to the top and just sit there. I would go into a fantasy world at times, of a whole other life like having family dinners, watching TV, family outings, going for walks, playing games, and just enjoying each other. It would have been so nice. I would just sit there for hours and mentally leave this world.

There was a gang way by my house, and it was boarded up, but I knew how to get in. I would use the bathroom there because I did not want to go into my house. I would walk around the neighborhood feeling lost, and I would talk to anyone and everyone, telling stories of how I would like my life to be, and it just made things easier to pretend like I had a normal life. One time, close to where my friend lived, we made a small house made of cardboard. We used to play card games, playhouse, and sometimes we just talked.

I went to that house after one of the incidents, and I remember I got into trouble because my mom was looking for me and could not find me. When I was inside the box, I would feel like I was the only person in the world, and no one could hurt me. Minds have good way of blocking things. My mind had to grow up fast. The child in me died early on. I wish I could remember all of the good, but I only remember some. I try not to dig. God's grace and mercy helped me to survive. I remember one time, watching my mom cook. I put a sheet over our kitchen table and made a tent. I pretended we had a perfect world. My mom and I would talk about school and little things that were going on with my friends. We pretended that everything was okay. My mom did not show her feelings, but I knew she was not happy, but in that moment, we were happy.

We went on vacation to a revival camp in Missouri, and we visited Jesse James's hideaway cave. I liked it at the cave. It was beautiful inside. It had all these pretty colors of ice hanging in the cave. You could hear your voice echo in there. I was talking to so many different people. I just got lost in this new world I entered. For a couple of hours, I was a normal kid. I enjoyed looking at all the items in the souvenir store. I could have spent my whole vacation there, but we had to go back to the campgrounds. The meetings were held under the tent, and it was like an outside church.

When there were no meetings, we were able to go swimming. We had a cabin we stayed in, but I only remember bits and pieces of it. My dad even mess with me while we were there. I would stand in the shower and cry (because I felt alone). While at the revival camp, my mom attended three to four times a day, and they were very long. I would walk around the campgrounds feeling lost and confused. I just couldn't understand why he had to bother me there also. I felt angry, and I believe I started to get mad at God because every time I needed my mom, she was at some church meeting.

At a certain point, everyone was looking for me because I took a walk, and I just kept walking. I wasn't running away, but I just wanted to disappear. When they found me, I told them I was going to the corner store and got lost. I remember all of that about the vacation, but I still can't quite remember my parents very well. I remember them at the cave but only a glimpse of a memory. I felt evil present, even on vacation because the presence of evil was with my dad. Wherever he was, evil was there too. I remember after an incident, I felt threatened and dirty. I remember being in the cabin and just crying while he was hurting me, but no one came to help.

My mom was always at the meetings. I felt abandoned by her. Crazy as it sounds, I just wanted to go home or, better yet, back to the cave. There was an area above the shower rooms that they use to eat in or have small meetings. I used to like to sit in there by myself, and I could hear the music and just relax.

I have a picture of my mom and dad at the field museum in Chicago. If I did not have that picture, I would not remember him being there. I do remember my mom being there. I do have one memory of him though, and we were going on the coal miner's ride. It was so cool. I enjoyed the tour guide telling the story of the coal miners. Things like that always took my mind away from reality. My mom used to love going to see the silent movies they had at the field museum. I thought they were cool, and I enjoyed watching them too. I liked watching my mom laugh. I couldn't tell you if my dad was there or not to save my life. I would hold my mom's hand, and we would laugh at the movie. I believe it was her way of coping also.

One day, my dad got so angry with me because as I got older, I started fighting back. He chased me up the stairs and to the end of the porch and had me in the corner. He started to choke me and tried to throw me over the banister. Thank God he snapped out of it and let me go. Some days I wished he would have, but God had different plans for me.

Every Christmas, my mom would put out a miniature Christmas town. It's my connection to a perfect world. No pain and no tears. I would sit and look at it and imagine different scenarios. I look at the kids and imagine them playing and having fun and not being ready to cry at any moment. I set up families and let my imagination go. Then I started with my own towns when I got older. Oh, how I never realized the depth of my thinking and why I was always making my little towns grow until I started this book. I have a miniature and a country town and a big one that goes on my coffee table, but I am working on only having the one on my coffee table, and I'm cutting it half. All of them perfect towns. This continues today, and I am slowly breaking it.

I did not have the life of a normal child. That was a domino effect for many dark years to follow.

This chapter is about the start of what the devil wanted to be my downfall, but it actually led to my victory! I say that because the events that happened when I was a little girl made a path for my decisions as I grew up. My father started to sexually abuse me from the time I can remember. As an abused person, I knew I never wanted to afflict the negativity or nightmare I went through as a child on someone else, so I went the wild way. Some people go the route of becoming an abuser.

I felt like I was given a life sentence. I wanted freedom so bad. I didn't know how to express the pain, shame, and fear I felt. So I looked for love (a father's love), a love that would take almost forty years to find. I was shown the love of my heavenly Father a few times and was not ready to believe or surrender to a love I didn't understand. I felt that religion was tainted as my father was a minister. I had no trust in people or the church. I didn't know the meaning of a real relationship with my heavenly Father.

When my mother used to go to her prayer meetings, I would beg her to take me with her, but she didn't listen, and she didn't realize, plus there was no childcare there. So I will not put it all on her. There was one night I'll never forget. I begged her not to leave, but she thought I just wanted attention, and she went to her prayer meeting. I didn't want to be left with that monster. After she left, he put me in the corner behind the closet door and made me face the wall. I kept crying, and then I felt that belt. He was telling me to never act like that again. Then he removed my clothes and touched me all over, telling me I was born to be his toy. I was nothing but a rag doll to him. I couldn't face my mom when she came home, so I acted like I was sleep. All the time I just wanted to cry "look what he did," but I didn't because I didn't want to hurt her.

As I got older, I loved my mom, but I was more hurt than angry at her. I just didn't understand why she didn't protect me, but I know she went through her own hell with him. I just didn't witness it all.

I used to go to summer camp with the church. It was so much fun. We used to go swimming, horseback riding, and canoeing. I felt like a real child. One summer when I was away at camp, she put him out. My mom couldn't take the abuse from him anymore. She had some idea that something was happening to me but wasn't sure. I was around ten years old, and it was too late because he had hurt me to a point of no turning back. He stole my innocence and my entire childhood. She never pressed charges because I never told her the details. I guess in my own way I wanted to protect her. I, later, was told that he had an affair with a lady from the church and later married her and had a child, who he also abused (allegedly). I was told she pressed charges against him and was sent to jail. I'm not sure how true that was, but I felt cheated and enraged that what he did to me was bypassed and gone unpunished, but he will one day stand in judgment for what he did.

The abuse took place mainly in the basement where no one could see or hear my cry. I felt alone and ashamed. That place to this day gives me the creeps when I think of it, but it has no hold on me. (Thank you, Jesus!) It was so demonic down there. The stairs were old and creaky, and he used to like to hide under them and jump out at me. It placed fear so deep down in me. My mom would have me get the sheets or clothes that were hanging up in the basement to put away. There were three ropes that were stretched out to hang the laundry, and so many times he would be right there behind the laundry. He was like a stalker. Till this day, I get a creepy feeling when I see laundry hanging. When I grew up and got an apartment, I could never go into the laundry room for fear of being raped, so I would go to a public laundry mat. I could never sleep in a completely dark room for fear of someone sneaking up on me. I was forty-four before I could sleep without a closet light.

My father used to work at a garage that fixed cars. I used to like to go there. It was nice when I could be with my dad, and he wasn't hurting me. One of the workers or owners used to live upstairs, and it was so cool. The patio was on the roof and lead into the house. He had a son a little older than me. I used to like to go there until my father did what he did. He sold me like I was cheap garbage. His friend used to joke that his son and I would get married. So he wanted his son to be able to see what he was getting. I remember hearing this conversation, and I went on the roof and hid behind a door. My father came out there and got me. I was crying, begging him not to do this to me. He took me inside and handed me over to his friend and his son. I thought it was only going to be the son, but his father joined in. Needless to say, the only thing that was not done to me was intercourse. Thank God.

When it was over and we were walking to the bus stop, I remember my father holding my hand tight, saying, "You must never tell anyone." It would kill your mother to know the trashy things her daughter does. I was only eight. All I want to know was why. *Why would you do this to me? It was bad enough you did things to me, but to sell me for a cheap thrill?* Now I know it exposed me to a lot of demonic spirits that would manifest in my adult life. Quite honestly, I did not even start to deal with the pain of this until I started writing my book. Thank God I have been taught how to pray and I know who I am in Christ. "God created man in his own image" (Genesis 1:27). Not saying the tears have not fallen because they have. Tears release pain. It's not healthy to hold pain in, and God wants us to be set free.

I had a silent cry that no one heard. The sexual acts that my father made me do were unbearable. That when I became an adult, I used sex as a weapon to get what I wanted. It became a tool for me to get love, money, alcohol, drugs, etc.

When I look at pictures of my dad now, I see the emptiness in him. I have one good childhood memory. We went for ice cream on a warm sunny day, and we were walking down the street, and he was holding my hand. There was no threat, just a father's love. I often wonder why he could not be like that all the time, but I now know he allowed demons to run his life. I often wonder what happened to him as a child. That generational curse *stops* with me!

One day when I was around eleven, after my dad was no longer living in house, my mom had me get the laundry as always not knowing how scared I was to go down there, but this is one of those days the devil tried to get control my mind. (Except now I have the tools to cast him out of my mind and speak the word of God to him and my mind.) Although my dad was no longer living in our house, he knew how to get into the basement. So when I went downstairs, my father was sitting on a chair inside of a pentagram made of chalk. He had a robe on and just looked at me and said, "You are the daughter of Satan." I cannot even begin to express the fear and terror that came over me. I ran upstairs screaming. I told my mom what happened, and she went downstairs, but he went out the back door. It was a statement that took my identity that would take my whole life to get back. *For I am a child of God, Jesus Christ, my Lord and Savior.*

For months after he was gone, there was a bad smell in the pantry that my mother could not get rid of, and then she found a bottle that said "Hail Satan" on it. She had the church come and do a cleanse on our house. I found out later that my father was a Satan worshiper (a.k.a. minister). There was one time that my dad tried to choke my mother, and she rebuked him in the name of Jesus and started speaking in tongues. He had no choice but to let her go and leave. The blood of Jesus was too powerful for him. That was the only time I witness him hurting her.

By the time my mom found out and understood everything (I was sixteen when I told her the truth), it was too late. The damage was done. I started messing around with boys at the age of twelve. There was no sex, but I was doing things that a normal twelve-year-old should not be doing or knowing. This was the start of many males that came into my life. From twelve to seventeen, I was on the path of destruction. Sex and drinking took over, and I was hanging out with an older crowd. Hanging around an older crowd made drinking easier. Some of the older men that I hung out with are still in my life to this day. The reasons and purposes have changed over the years. I took the negatives and turned them into positives.

I did try to have some kind of a normal teenage life away from what I was doing in the streets. I was in dance class, and I also was in gymnastic. When I would dance, I would feel so free. I felt important. Gymnastics just took me to a whole new level of knowing that my body could be used for something great and not hurtful, but I got pregnant in my fallopian tube at sixteen. The surgery ended what I was trying to do good for me. I just wanted to be normal.

I used to feel that there were years of my childhood that were blocked from my mind. I used to want to know what they were. I thought that was the only way I could be set free, but what I learned in my recovery class at church is that we remember everything we just don't want to deal with it. It was a tactic from the enemy to keep me from my freedom. For years I felt like something worse happened to me, but as soon as I heard that in class, I felt years of chains break off me. Now I can focus on what happened and not a lie from the devil. I spent many years trying to remember something that didn't happen and spent so much time fighting demons that I will no longer give any more room in my mind, heart, and soul. I've learned how to cast out every demonic thing my father did to me and send it right back to the pits of hell where it belongs.

I dealt with fear for so long that I got tired of being afraid at every little noise and losing sleep that one day at the top of my stairs, I screamed, "Fear, you don't own me. I rebuke you in the name of Jesus, and you go back to the pits of hell where you belong. You cannot touch me, and you cannot control my life any longer!" Mind you, this happened while I was writing this book. From that day forward, I have learned how to deal with fear when it tries to creep in, and I can say *I am free*! I was fifty-one when this happened. I have learned how to walk with my protector every minute of the day.

My father once told me that he wishes I was never born. I used to agree, but now I have no regrets. I was born and went through this nightmare to help other women. "The spirit of the Lord is upon me, he has anointed me to preach to the poor, He has sent me to heal the brokenhearted, to proclaim liberty to the captives, and recovery of sight to the blind, to set at liberty those who are oppressed" (Luke 4:18).

I was told over and over that I never did anything wrong and that it was all his fault. That did not take away the shame and dirty feelings that I had. Only God could do that and break these walls down. Now that I am 100 percent open to him, these walls are crumbling down under my feet. Now I can dance on them with freedom and holiness. "Let all rejoice who put their trust in you, let them shout for joy Because you defend them, those who love your name be joyful in you. For you O Lord will bless the righteous; With favor you will surround, him as with a shield" (Psalms 5:11–12).

CHAPTER 2

Hurt on Top of Hurt

Unfortunately, my father was not the only abuser. He was just the start of a very painful beginning. When I was around eleven or twelve, my aunt molested me. It was presented to me as in a way that I thought I was doing a good thing. See, my uncle was gone for long periods of time on the weekends, so I would help with my younger cousins. I loved going over there. We use to watch movies and talk. I really cared about her, and that's what made it easy for her to use my trust for her demons.

One night, my aunt was drinking, and she had me try what she was drinking. Can't say I didn't like it or the way it was making me feel. We were listening to music, talking, and just having fun. We went in her bedroom, and she started trying on different items that she slept in. She wanted to see which one I liked. It was her way of making me feel comfortable, I guess. After that, I took a bath and got into bed like I always did, but this time was different. Normally I slept with my aunt in her bed while my uncle was gone to keep her company. She started to explain to me how lonely she was and began to show me what she would use to pleasure herself while my uncle was gone. I was curious as to how it felt. She began to show me how to use these toys. She had me use them on her to make her feel good, and then she used it on me. I knew it was wrong, but I was too scared to tell her to stop, and the alcohol was making me feel some kind of way. I didn't want to hurt her feelings. So I just never spent the night there again. I would avoid her at family functions.

My mom couldn't figure out why I didn't want to hang out there anymore. She thought that maybe my cousins and I didn't get along anymore. This is what they mean by a silent cry. I understand this statement all too well. Later on, I was relieved when my uncle divorced her. I was told that the reason that he divorced her was due to her drinking. She is one of many that I had to forgive. Forgiving people is one of the biggest steps to being set free and for healing to begin, but this didn't happen until I was in my late forties. "Father forgive them for they know not what they do" (Luke 23:34).

When I was around fifteen, I told my mom I needed some help, so she took me to a Christian therapist that did more damage than good. You see, during a session, I was crying, and he gave me a hug and started touching me. He told me that I was overreacting, and that's what adults do. I couldn't believe this was happening. Was he right? Was this normal? I pushed him away and ran out his office. My mom was outside, and I told her I was never coming back here, that it was a mistake to talk about it, and that I wasn't ready. I never told her the truth. I was done with God and the church. My head was spinning.

I was sixteen but had a mindset as if I was twenty-six. I was using alcohol as a tool to heal myself. I was looking everywhere for love except for up. I looked at all types of men—married or single. It didn't matter. I just would not mess with a friend's man. Somehow I managed to maintain some morals. I was out of control and still could not find the love I needed. As I stated in the last chapter, I got pregnant in my fallopian tube and was not able to have my baby. You see, I wanted that baby. I wanted someone to love me with no hesitation, someone that would not hurt me, but God knew I wasn't ready for a baby. I will see my baby one day in heaven.

I was going to school in the day and drinking at night. I learned from an early age how to be a functioning alcoholic. I looked older and was able to get into night clubs. I've always found it to be funny but sad that no one carded me until after I turned twenty-one. I enjoyed drinking. I felt good and had the courage to sleep with different men, but the truth was when it wore off and I remembered the stuff I did, I felt worse about me. It only took the pain away for a moment, and it also added pain. So I drank more.

When I was a sophomore in high school, I had a best friend who sometime was not home when I came over. (We didn't have cell phones like now.) So I found myself around her father a few times, and he was very charming and made me feel beautiful, and we ended up dating for a while. We had sex a few times. I finally told him this wasn't right. He didn't fight me on it, and I let my friendship die out. Between my sophomore years and my senior years, there was many men. I say *men* because I didn't mess with anyone my age. My mind was to grown, and they didn't do anything for me. I guess you can say I could have had a lot of guys going to jail, but no one really looked at me as a teenager. I wished my mother hadn't trust me so much. She had to work, and I played.

I hated high school, and I stuck to myself. I do not like cliques, which school had a lot of. So my mom let me go to night school my last year of high school so I could get better help with my grades. That's where I met my son's father. We dated for a while, and I was calming down. I asked him to get me pregnant, and I got pregnant, and we got married. I was in love, and I was going to have a baby that would love me unconditional. I was finally with one guy. It was perfect until I said I do. Then the physical abuse started. So now I was being abused in another form. We were in the car the first time he hit me. He was saying mean things to me, and I yelled at him. Before I knew it, he backslapped me. It really blew my mind.

We ended up living with his grandparents because he had a cocaine habit that I did not know about until he took all our money, and we lost are apartment. The abuse got worse, and his grandparents never said anything. After all, his grandpa treated his grandma like she was a servant.

One afternoon, he went to the store which was at the corner of the block, and he didn't come back until four in the morning. I guess I wasn't supposed to say anything, but I did, and he took my head and banged it on the corner of the fan and busted it open. I remember lying in bed, crying and holding my son. I promised my son I would get him out of there. I couldn't take no more slaps, no more kicks, and no more black eyes. I stayed to myself, except for my next-door neighbor who I was friends with and the only one I could talk to, but I would later find out she had an affair with him. So her telling me to leave him was not because she cared, but because she wanted him and thought she would change him. They later got married, and he treated her the same way. Because of her, it has taken me a long time to trust females.

I packed up my stuff and left, and my mom hid me at one of her friend's house from church. Then I called this guy I met on new year's (my next husband). We ended up dating. I was able to get a divorce easily from my previous husband because he never showed up for court. I had my beautiful son and a new man.

CHAPTER 3

Covering up the Hurt with Marriage

As I stated earlier, I met my next husband on New Year's Eve of '87. I was around twenty-one years old. He helped me with my son. We moved in with his family until we could get a place of our own. When we got our place, we got married, and I had my second child, my sweet little angel.

One thing my father stole from me was breastfeeding. I could never do it; it felt dirty to me. I thought it was supposed to come naturally, but it didn't. I feel like I lost a big part of motherhood.

For the first five years, the marriage was good. We were doing things as a family. We were going to church, and things were changing. Going to church was slowly changing things. I stopped drinking and became a dedicated wife and mother. My family was everything to me.

Over the years, I started noticing that there was something that did not sit very well with me. His temper. I didn't understand it. I kept a clean house and cooked. I was always home. It didn't seem good enough. He wanted perfection. I could not take being yelled at for the small things all the time. I knew that I should have left when my kids were young, but I didn't. I thought that if I didn't show the hurt around my kids, then they would be okay. I was wrong. That was the worst mistake I made. Staying in an abusive marriage whether it is verbal or physical is very unhealthy. Thinking that staying for the kids is a good thing but isn't. Children pick up on everything good or bad no matter how much you try to hide it.

He did play favors with the kids. Even though he adopted my son, I don't think he ever really accepted him as his son. He had a horrible temper with him, but my daughter was daddy's little girl, which, in the end, hurt both my children. My son felt left out, and my daughter felt abandoned because after I put him out, he did nothing with his children.

We went to counseling for a while through the church. I was told to stand by his side while he was working through his problems. This was very hard for me to do because things were not getting better. They were getting worse. The church said he was not right, but it would be wrong for me to leave him. So I left the church. Things were getting worse and now becoming violent. We started going to a different church, and now I was getting counseling again. I could not take it anymore. My counselor and I became friends. She was also having serious problems with her marriage but didn't tell anyone. I could not understand how a couple that was in the church, fighting, drinking, and listening to worldly music could be counselors in the church. I know now that I should have gone to my pastor. I did not seek God. I made my own choices. I left the church and went back to worldly thinking. I kicked him out and went back to my view of men.

After I kicked him out, he started stalking me. He would show up at my job, hang around my house, and threaten to kill me numerous of times to the point that I bought a gun. It took me two years to get a divorce from him. Every time we would go to court, he would tell me he wasn't going to sign the papers. (That's a nice way to put it.) Finally, the judge gave me one. I think he felt sorry for me. I was so angry and hurt, but I think more disappointed. Now I had to figure out how to raise my kids by myself because he refused to help in any kind of way. I took him to court for child support, which he still owes me till this day. I just washed my hands of him and took care of my kids myself.

CHAPTER 4

Wolf in Sheep's Clothing

With all the hurt that was piled on year after year, I shut down emotionally. During this time, I gave up on God, marriage, and love. Then I met a man that I called my husband. (We were not married legally.) We were together for ten years. We took vows just between us. He wore my ring, and I wore his. He was my protector from my last husband. Somehow, some way I allowed him to control me. He was able to control who I talked to, what I wore, and the air I breathed. We were together most of the time, but when we were not, it did not bother me because I knew he loved me. (At least I thought it was love.) He mainly stayed because of his daughter. Oh yeah, did I mention he was legally married?

He was an easygoing smooth talker, and everyone loved him. That is how I got sucked in. He was my protector against my ex-husband who was constantly threatening my life. He was the one who gave me the money to buy a gun. He became a man that I would do anything for. He was that protector that comes in like a knight in shining armor. He was really a wolf in sheep's clothing that the Bible warns us against. "Beware of false prophets, who come to you in sheep's clothing but inwardly are ravenous wolves" (Matthew 7:15).

He had a lifestyle that I became accustomed to. He started dealing drugs and would take me on exchanges. On one of his exchanges, he was asked why I was brought along. He responded, "She is my security," and that I would shoot someone in between their eyes faster than they could blink for him. That part was true. I was the one holding the gun, making sure that nothing went wrong. I was his ride-or-die chick. Literally. By this time, I was popping Vicodin, and sometimes I would smash them up and snort them. I needed to use more and more to chase away the boogieman. See some people can't handle having one thing done to them, which I get, but I had one thing after another from the time I was able to remember. I couldn't take it anymore.

At this time, the devil had such a hold on me and used this man to keep me in this dark world. I did not know if I was coming or going. I was getting deeper and deeper in a world that I did not want to be a part of. He didn't love me; he was just grooming me to do whatever he wanted. I had no self-worth. I had a lot of game though. I understand the statements for the love of money, sex, drugs, and rock and roll (minus the rock and roll); it's a big game out in the streets. I played it well. When they say fast money goes fast, that's exactly what they mean. I can't tell you where any of that money went to.

One night, I went out with some ladies I really didn't know for long, and we went to a club downtown. Needless to say, I drank a lot. "My husband" called and said he was coming to get me. So the ladies left without me (instead of waiting until he got there). In the meantime, I was just talking, dancing, and drinking with different people. I was dancing with this one girl, and we were talking and laughing, then I noticed her looking at this one guy, and she nodded her head, and so did he. Being in the streets, I luckily had a lot of street-smart tips. I told her, "Whatever you're on, I'm not about that life." I went to the bathroom and called him. I told him what was going on, and he told me to stay in the bathroom and wait for him because he was just around the corner. So I did. It wasn't until I got ready to send this book off that God told me to put this in. He also showed me that it wasn't a threesome they were interested in; they were traffickers. I wasn't sure, but I do know every time I think about that night, I get horrible feelings and just thank God for protecting me. Maybe after this book, my children will understand why I am the way I am. In their eyes, I'm scared of everything. It's not that, I'm just overly cautious.

I didn't realize how much he was abusing me until he was out of my life. This abuse was different and was done in a way that was unfamiliar to me. It was not done out of anger, but it was very controlled. He had me convinced that what he was doing was out of love. He only wanted to see me happy because he loved me, and I believed him. I was led to believe that abuse was to be scary and full of anger. This was not the case with him. That is why it was so easy to believe him. When I saw how much he enjoyed me being happy, I wanted to give more of myself to this lifestyle for him. After about six months, I was going on the drug runs for him. I was very good at hiding the drinking and the drug abuse from my kids. The kids were older, and I don't think they ever questioned us and our relationship status because he was always around.

My heart was so heavy, and I felt that I was no good for my kids anymore. I loved them so much, but I felt I was just ruining their life. I wrote each one of my kids a letter and my mother and godparents and explained how sorry I was, but I couldn't do life anymore. I got in the tub, had some drinks, and I had my gun. Before I knew it, he was walking in the bathroom and dropped to his knees and begged me to give him the gun, that he loved me, and my kids needed me.

As soon as he said *my kids*, I broke and handed him the gun. He pulled me out of the tub and held me, and I just cried. We talked for a while, and I never did tell him he was one of my biggest problems. He knew some of what my dad did, so he thought that was what was wrong with me. After he put me to bed, he left and took the gun with him. I was no longer allowed to hold on to it. So I went on with life and all the hurt insides. Even though I was still hurting, God used him to save my life. "Nevertheless the Lord your God would not listen to Balaam, but the Lord your God turned the curse into a blessing for you, because the Lord your God *loves* you" (Deuteronomy 23:5).

I don't understand how his real wife didn't know. I have a feeling that she did and did not question it or just ignored it. I was comfortable with my life until he went to jail for three years. During those three years, I stuck by his side. But since he was gone and I had no man around abusing me, I was able to realize I needed to get out. My eyes started to open up, but I tried to fight it. "Open my eyes, that I may see wondrous things from your law" (Psalms 119:18).

I did not want to come to the realization that things were changing. When he got out, he was full of anger. He wanted to go back to making more deals. At this point, I wanted no parts of this. He started going back to the streets, and he was doing it without me. I was at the point where I started praying him out of my life. Every time I packed his stuff to kick him out, he would convince me to unpack it and told me that I was crazy. He used to tell me all the time that he was not going anywhere. I cried out to God for help every time.

One night, when he was not around, my phone rang. It was his wife. Her calling me made me laugh. It was a laugh of freedom. We talked for long time. I was so grateful that this day came. I had a chance to apologize to her and asked her for forgiveness. The relationship ended. The lie was finally brought to light. Once that happened, it no longer holds its ground. "For nothing is secret that will not be revealed, nor anything hidden that will not be known and come to light" (Luke 8:17).

I was finally free of him and the life I had with him. God will always provide a way out. "No temptation has overtaken you except such as is common to man; but God is faithful, who will not allow you to be tempted beyond what you are able, but with the temptation will also make the way of escape, that you may be able to bear it" (1 Corinthians 10:13). The protection that I found in this man really came from God. "Hear my cry, O God Attend to my prayer" (Psalms 61:1). God did attend to my prayer. I just can't thank him enough.

It made me think about how many times that God protected me, how many times I could have gone to jail for a long time, and how many car accidents I could have been in driving drunk or high. Thank you, thank you, thank you, Jesus, for your protection. I do pray for him and his family. I pray that someone will come across his path and help him get delivered. Something bad had to have happened to him in order to feel like he needs to be superior and controlling of someone. I know now that he didn't love me. His demons did. I was so messed up his demons were able to feed from my hurt. As far as demons are concerned, we were the perfect match, but God did not want that life for me. He had a life of freedom and peace waiting for me.

My heavenly Father is so awesome. He had me in the palm of his hands the whole time. Some of you might say, "Well, if that's true, why did he allow all of this to happen?" You see, I had a choice on what I said yes and no to. What I went through can now be used to help others. As a child, I didn't, but my father did, and he chose wrong. God has healed me from the wrong that was done to me. The devil tried to destroy me. God stepped in and said, "Not my child."

CHAPTER 5

A Different Level of Hurt

Well, I thought that the best way to get over a man was to get with another one. That is one of the biggest lies that I have ever heard. The truth is you need to take time to heal yourself. I never did this. I would just change what I was doing or the type of man I would be with. This had a tendency to backfire on me.

I met this guy who was the total opposite of my exes, and it was nice at first, but I wanted to move ahead and make something of our lives. He was in a rut and wanted to stay in rut. He didn't know how to let go of things or people from his past. So when I found out he was still talking to his ex, I was done. I wanted change, and I had begun having a zero tolerance to being hurt. I was going to be happy one way or the other.

I gave up two years of my life I was still going nowhere. I ended the relationship for many reasons. He is a good man, but not the man for me. He also had a lot to be healed from. So I took a break for a year from having a relationship, just not men. Also, not a good idea.

At another New Year's party, that's right another New Year's (haha), when I saw him, I knew that he was perfect for me. He swept me off my feet, and what was supposed to be a one-night stand turned into the best year and half of my life. I was finally happy and felt very protected. His smile made everything okay. I know now that God had me in his life to make the last of his life happy. He told me one time that no one has ever made him as happy as I did, and that challenged him to be a better man. We had plans for the future romantically and business.

On the night of June 28, 2013, after I had talked to him on the phone, I got a phone call from his sister that he was on life support, and he may not make it. I flew to the hospital. When I got there, his family was sitting in the waiting room. They said the doctors were waiting for his leg to get a blood clot so it would stop bleeding. They said if it did, they could save his life, but he would lose his leg. I remember sitting in prayer to God to save him, and I gave my word I would take care of him. I went to see him with his uncle and his mom, and when I came in the room and saw that big machine, I was terrified.

Being in the health field, I knew too much, and what was going on with the machines, I knew it wasn't good. I leaned into him and said, "You cannot leave me. You said this was the beginning of us, and you have two kids to fight for." I told him I loved him, and a tear fell out of his left eye. I know he heard me. Then they had me leave the room because his blood pressure was dropping. We went back to wait, and then the doctor came in, and I saw it all over her face. I couldn't move, and his poor mother fell to the ground. They brought us back to see him, and his sister gave me a chair to sit down by his face. I couldn't cry, I couldn't scream, and I was numb. I kept thanking him for loving me. The last thing he said to me was, "Okay, my lady, I'll call you when I get in the house. Love you." I never got that phone call. After he was murdered, my drinking really picked up. It was a pain I couldn't bear. I was no good for his mom or sons. I tried, but the pain was unbearable. I didn't know how to handle being around them without him. I had to pull away my drinking was out of control.

Once I gave my life back to Jesus, I had to forgive the man that killed him. With him being killed, I had to go to another level of forgiveness and prayer. I can tell you it wasn't easy, but forgiveness is a choice. I choose not to give his killer any power. I want to be able to remember his love, his laughter, his beautiful smile, and the way he loved his mother and children. I did not want to remember the bad. Now I can smile at the memories of him.

Then five months later, I lost my precious mother. I lost a lot of time with her in the last year of her life 'cause I was running from God. And the anointing that was on my mother convicted me every time I saw her. It was the Holy Ghost in her. It's taken a long time to get past this, and I'm still struggling some with my mom's death. I do thank God though that two weeks before she passed, we had dinner alone, and I had the best time I ever had with her. I know one day, God will completely heal me from her death and my family. You see, at my mother's funeral, most of my family didn't even acknowledged me. I found out around the time I had my kids that my father had African American blood in him. I've dealt with a lot of identity issues, and when I found this information out, a lot made sense to me. I always felt out of place and was treated like the black sheep of the family. I have a big family that don't even know me.

After eight months of him being gone, I met someone. Mistake, because I was nowhere near over his death. But my friends convinced me that I needed to at least try to move on. We lived together for a while, but it didn't work out because he was not ready to be in a relationship. I was so broken inside. He told me one time that he felt like he was in competition with someone who was dead, and he probably was right. He cheated on me, and that was it. Zero tolerance. I broke up with him, and three months later, I came running back to my heavenly Father. I was broken into a million pieces.

I have come to the point where I do not blame him for everything. I brought a lot of baggage to the relationship. Somehow I tried to make him have to make up for what everyone did. It doesn't work that way. You must heal yourself in between relationships. It's not fair to anyone when you don't. I had to ask him to forgive me, and he did as I forgave him. We can speak to each other kindly and care about each other's well-being. See, he had been hurt also. So two hurt people don't mix well. I wanted to save him. I had a mindset I could fix him. You cannot fix any one, they can only fix themselves. And the true help comes from Jesus.

CHAPTER 6

The Start of Freedom

Well, on a Wednesday evening, I went back to my home church. My pastor's wife saw me and remembered me after seventeen years. Wow! I can't even begin to explain what that meant to me. She got the pastor, and he also remembered me. Didn't question where I have been, he just asked if I was back home to stay. I said yes. I told him a couple of things that happened to me, and he prayed over me. I've been back for seven years now. I'm single and waiting on God to send me a husband that is in love with Jesus as I am. But until then, Jesus is the only man in my life. This has been the best seven years of my life. I'm sober and filled with the Holy Spirit. I've learned how to forgive and live. Please don't have the mindset that watching church on TV is the same as going to church (unless you're not able to get to church). I used to do that, and believe me, there is a *huge* difference. You also need to be in a church that teaches how to forgive, love, change the way you think, and have a pastor that teaches the Word the correct way and is dedicated to God.

Being free is easier than you think. Pray, believe what the Word says about you, and forgive. You must want to be free number 1. Trust me when I say the devil will mess with your mind as you are moving toward freedom. But with the word of God, you can break every chain that holds you bondage. "O Lord truly I am your servant; the son of your maidservant; You have loosed my bonds" (Psalm 116:16). "For the word of God is living and powerful, and sharper than any two-edged sword, piercing even to the division of soul and spirit, and of joints and marrow, and is a discerner of the thoughts and intents of the heart" (Hebrews 4:12). "He has redeemed my soul in peace from the battle that was against me, for there were many against me" (Psalms 55:18).

One of the most important things to do is get back to a Bible-teaching church. If it's your first time going, make sure the church is spirit-filled, believes in healing, teaches God's love for us, believes in speaking in tongues, the power of the blood, forgiveness, water baptism, and teaches how to have a relationship with God. Not religious acts. These are the gifts God has for us.

I'm so blessed to have a pastor that has taught me how to communicate with God and showed me how much he loves me. "Let the elders who rule well be counted worthy of double honor, especially those who labor in the word and doctrine" (1 Timothy 5:17). My God is not an angry God but full of love and mercy. He is my father, and nothing or no one can come between us. "Nor height nor depth, nor any other created thing, shall be able to separate us from the love of God which is in Christ Jesus our Lord) and (John 14:18 I will not leave you orphans; I will come to you" (Romans 8:39).

God put it on my heart to write a testimony to help others. Wasn't sure how to, but I started writing what has happened to me. One day, when going to the library to write, I had all my papers out and my Bible. This man came and sat on stool next to me and just stared at me. I felt so much fear and darkness. Nobody else was around where I was. I stood up and started packing my stuff. I looked over, and he was gone. I could not see where he went. I called my godmother and told her what was going on, and I walked to the front, and I was looking out the window to see if I could see him in the parking lot. I couldn't, and there was a crowd of people going out at the same time. So I told my godmother I was going to the car. She stayed on the phone with me until I got in the car.

After I got home, I was sitting on my bed, thinking about what happened, and I asked God what that was. He gave me a vision of the devil sitting on that stool. I could see him as clear as day. It gave me the chills, but I said from that day forward, I would finish my book if it only frees one person, it's worth it. It's taken me six years to do this. There was a part of my story I wanted to leave out. I didn't know how my children would react, and I didn't know how people would look at me. I was still dealing with shame. Shame has no hold on me anymore (when the enemy tries to remind me of my past, I remind him who I belong to and his future).

One night, at church, we had a conference going on. The preacher that was talking said, "There is someone writing a book, and you're leaving a chapter out. Without that chapter, you are not telling your whole story." I fell forward and was holding my stomach. It was like an arrow hit me, and I knew God was talking directly to me. I won't lie putting how low I went in this book was not easy, but I must be obedient to God. I've come to a point in my life that I will not allow anyone to hold my past over my head or against me. If you truly cannot forgive or let go, the only thing for me to do is put that person in God's hands and keep living and love. I will not live like a victim. I am free, and that is how I am going to live. As I wrote this book, I felt layers of pain coming off. I thank God for freedom.

CHAPTER 7

The Fight with Fear

A lot of what I dealt with was fear, self-worth, codependency, and unforgiveness. Fear is a big form of bondage. I constantly felt like something was going to happen. I lost a lot of sleep because of fear. I became a very light sleeper and would hear every little noise. I had to check every window and door over and over before I could fall asleep. I didn't know how to trust God to protect me. "He said to them, why are you so fearful? How is it that you have no faith?" (Mark 4:40).

Now when I feel like that, I put the blood of Jesus over me and my home. I've learned how to have peace. "But I will sing of your power; Yes, I will sing aloud of your mercy in the morning; For you have been my defense and refuge the day of my trouble" (Psalms 59:16). "So we may boldly say; The Lord is my helper; I will not fear. What can man do to me?" (Hebrews 13:6). "For God has not given us a spirit of fear, but of power and of love and of a sound mind" (2 Timothy 1:7). I know now that God did this threw baby steps.

Seven years ago was the first time I ever lived on the first floor in an apartment. At times, I would be afraid, and other times I would be okay. This was around the time I went back to church. I started to trust God, and fear became less and less in my life. Then I decided to move closer to the church. I really wanted to buy, but God wasn't done with me. I ended up renting a townhouse. It took me two weeks before I could sleep upstairs in my bed. I was sleeping on the couch.

The first time I slept in my bed was in the middle of the day. I wanted to take a nap. It felt so scary having two floors under me, and I couldn't see what was going on. The devil was really working on my mind, but this time I was learning how to fight back. Then I heard this song about getting over fear, and it help me so much. "The Breakup Song" by Francesca Battistelli. One night, when I couldn't sleep, I stood at the top of my stairs and screamed, "Fear, you don't own me. I rebuke you in the name of Jesus." When I said this, I felt years of chains fall off me. I was fifty when this happened. This was the first step of being free.

The second step was taking my identity back. I am a child of God, and fear has no place in my life. Fear will keep you in bondage. It can control a lot in your life, sometimes not even knowing it. Knowing that I am a child of God means I have a Father that will never hurt me. I feel real protection for the first time.

The third step is praising God for freedom. Every time I feel fear try to pop, back up, and trust me, the enemy will try. I say, "Lord, I thank you for my deliverance," and I tell fear, "In the name of Jesus, you must and will leave me alone." As I said, God was healing me in baby steps. First, the apartment and then the townhouse, which has a washer and dryer in the basement. I've learned through writing this book that fear has controlled my life in all kinds of ways. Not being able to travel, not going to different events, etc. So I asked God to show me what was still hidden inside. Some hurts are so embedded and have been there for so long. You don't realize it until you start peeling away layers of hurt. So I pray for healing and forgiveness of any people and events that I don't remember but have caused damaged to me.

Forgiveness is very important. It not only sets you free, but it also sets others free as well. When we don't forgive, it hurts our health and turns into bitterness. Forgiveness is a decision to let go of what someone has done to you. It no way means you have to continue a relationship with them, or that you forget, and it definitely does not excuse them of what they did. "Pursue peace with all people, and holiness, without which no one will see the lord: Looking carefully lest anyone fall short of the grace of God; lest any root of bitterness springing up cause trouble and by this many become defiled" (Hebrews 12:14–15). It just starts to rebuild you. There's a freedom that makes your spirit light.

Something I didn't have for a long time was self-worth. If we don't have self-worth, it can lead to pride, which is a defense mechanism when we feel bad about ourselves. People have a tenancy to talk about things that they have done in order to feel good about themselves. It's like getting a pat on the back. Pride doesn't come from God. "For all that is in the world-the lust of the flesh, the lust of the eyes and the pride of life-is not of the Father but is of the world" (1 John 2:16). "Everyone proud in heart is an abomination to the Lord; Though they join forces, none will go unpunished" (Proverbs 16:5).

Pride will open the door to many spirits. In order to get past pride, we need to instead give God praise and thank him for giving us a blessing or the wisdom to conquer are shortcomings. God wants us to have a spirit of meekness. "Seek the Lord, all you meek of the earth, who have upheld His justice. Seek righteousness, seek humility. It may be that you will be hidden in the day of the Lord's anger" (Zephaniah 2:3). "Blessed are the meek, for they shall inherit the earth" (Matthew 5:5).

When we learn how to not let what a person has done to us be the level of our value, we can turn the hurt channel to the healing channel. Know that God is in control, not the people or person that has hurt you. "These things I have spoken to you, that in Me you may have peace. In the world you will have tribulation; but be if good cheer, I have overcome the world" (John 16:33).

When we don't deal with pride, it can result in lying, anger, mood swings, shyness, bragging, a unforgiving spirit, and being bitter.

CHAPTER 8

Moving Forward

My story is one of hundreds of women or men that have been abused. Abuse at a young age can lead to a dark path in life.

You see, as children, we learn from the ones we love. This can go two ways. We can learn how love should be, or we can learn the opposite. If we are shown how to love incorrectly, it sets us up for our behavior in the future. By God's grace, we can overcome and remain the victor. Unfortunately, the incorrect love that we have been shown may lead us to live a disruptive life. As I once did, but by his grace, I am free. I am free to be the woman that God has intended me to be and fulfill my destiny. He has redeemed my life in peace from the battle that was against me. God has turned things around and healed me. He has also taught me how to forgive so that I can receive my blessing. But you must read the Bible and be in church to hear his word in order to start healing. I am not against counseling, but my advice is if you feel something is not right, say something. If you are getting it from church, please go to your pastor. Don't leave the church.

First and foremost, God should be your counselor. It should not stop there. Regular counselors let you tell your story. Letting go is needed if it is done in a healthy way. Holding it all in will keep you captive. This is what Satan wants. Once you're free, you can start to live the life that God has intended for you. I have wasted so many years not living God's way. This caused me to stay connected to my pain, which in turn made things more difficult for me to get over.

I did not know what hurt to attack first. Once you have acknowledged that it's time to get rid of the pain, you can start to peel back layers and begin to heal. The chains will break as layers are peeled away. Address everything big or small that you can remember. Healing will take time, but trust God, and it will happen. Stay focused on what is in front of you. When you look at the past, it can pull you back. The important things are to look forward and work on getting set free from the hurt. Hurt is so damaging.

I have learned that anger is a cover up for hurt. For many years, I was angry. I was labeled as having a bad temper. I used to lash out at people about things that could easily be fixed or talked about. I would never accept the fact that I may have been wrong and blew things out of proportion to prove my point. I was angry at people who hurt me, including myself. I was ashamed and hated myself for things I did, things I allowed, and things I did to myself. People at work also labeled me this way. I became very protective of things that were important to me. I did not care what people thought of me as long as people left me alone. It was a way of protecting me from the world and not letting people in.

Years ago, it was easy for me to fly off the handle. I had gone through so much that I was like a boiling pot flowing over. It didn't take much for me to get upset. Now I realize that was my way of protecting myself. If I got mad, it would fuel a fire in me that would take me away from what was going on in my life. As I go on with Christ and read the Bible, I have peace over my past, and the pot that was boiling over is disappearing.

As I started to forgive people, I was less angry. I found myself feeling joy and smiling more. I have learned to stop myself before I get angry. I try to catch myself, take a breath, step back, and find out what is really bothering me. Sometimes I still get angry, and the devil loves to throw it in my face, so I throw it right back. I have learned how to control the spirit of pride and say "I'm sorry" to the person that made me angry. Whether I am right or wrong, there is always another way. All the years of drinking covered up and pushed down feeling that would still need to be worked out. Years of being with the wrong men caused even more pain. The only answer is the mercy, grace, love, and forgiveness of God. I've also learned that I needed to brake sexual soul ties. Everyone I've ever been with is attached to my soul, which needed to be broken from me. It healed be from the hurt from that relationship, whether I caused the hurt or they did.

It is good to make a list of the people that have hurt you. Figure out what part that hurt plays in your life and forgive. Praying for answers helps if you don't fully understand the role it played in your life and how it affected you. Ask God for understanding He will give you that understanding, and it may surprise you.

CHAPTER 9

A Bad Dream of Hope

I used to have a dream about walking around a pool. It was dark and had no walls. Around the pool, there was nothing but vines. The pool was filled with snakes, alligators, and dragons. The fear was unexplainable and bone-chilling. I would always wake up right before they pulled me in. I stopped having this dream for years. It wasn't until I started writing this book that I finally understood the dream. The pool was the lake of fire. The snakes, alligators, and dragons are the demons trying to destroy me.

When I would wake up, it was God's way of saving me. I have since rebuked that dream. Satan will not stop the work that God is doing in me. He will not stop the gift that God has given me to help others when I think of the dream. I feel no fear, and I have peace because I know God has me in his arms. "God is our refuge and strength, a very present help in trouble" (Psalm 46:1). He has kept me safe through all the things I have been through and done. I know he has not carried me this far to let me fall. His grace and love are forever. "Who has saved us and called us with a holy calling, not according to our works, but according to his own purpose and grace which was given to us in Christ Jesus before time began" (1 Timothy 1:9).

CHAPTER 10

The Past Is Being Undone

Drinking has done a lot of damage to my health. I am believing for full healing. Sometime when I talk, I forget or trip over my words. I have problems remembering, and it is a struggle for me to remember scripture verse and other things I try to memorize. You can tell me something, and a few minutes later, I won't be able to tell you what you said, but I know what you said if that makes any sense. I keep speaking over my mind that I have the mind of Christ. Lately, when I talk I'll remember a verse, and I get so excited. I know God is healing me.

My desire is to be able to spit the word of God out of my mouth without a thought to it. I know it's coming, and I declare it in the name of Jesus. When I was baptized, I left the old me in the water. I am a new person. "Therefore, if anyone is in Christ, he is a new creation; old things have passed away; behold, all things have become new" (2 Corinthians 5:17). My pastor's wife told me I have childlike faith. I like that.

At the time the disciples came to Jesus, saying, "Who then is greatest in the kingdom of heaven? Then Jesus called a little child to him, set him in the midst of them, and said, Assuredly, I say to you, unless you are converted and become as little children, you will by no means enter the kingdom of heaven. Therefore, whoever humbles himself as this little child is the greatest in the kingdom of heaven. Whoever receives one little child like this in my name receives me. (Matthew 18:1–5)

I do need to say that if you have a drinking or drug problem, please get help. It took many nights of crying out to God for help to stop. I would think about it at work and would tell myself no, but when I would be on my way home, I would stop and grab a drink and say, "I'll just have one." I would end up having three to four mixed drinks before the end of the night. When I got up in the morning, I would just cry to God and scream help me. It was a cycle I dealt with for a while, but with each drink, I started losing the taste for it. Then before I knew it, I didn't want it at all and developed a hate for it. He delivered me. I did attend recovery classes at church for a year. There is a lot of help out there. You don't have to do it alone. Trust me, God will walk with you. Get in your Bible. The Bible has over seven thousand promise to stand on.

I had trouble with smoking also. I got to the point where I was smoking for a day and not even smoking all of it. I wanted to quit so bad. On January 23, 2019, I almost lost my life because of them. The doctors were able to stop what they called a black-widow heart attack. They put a stent in my artery. On my way to the operating room, I felt Jesus walking with me and holding my hand. The day I was getting released, I cried out to God for help. I was afraid to get in my car and smell the cigarettes I begged for his help. I'll tell you that I haven't smoke a cigarette since. I don't crave them or want them. Sometimes the devil puts it in my mind how nice it would be to have a cigarette and a small drink. That it would be okay because I have it under control. As fast as those thoughts come is as fast as I cast them down. I want no part of what God delivered me from.

My life belongs to him, and I am just going the way he is showing me. He has been putting some awesome godly people in my life. I'm excited for what God has in stored for me. Don't know where I'm going, but I trust God, and I know wherever he sends me, he's right next to me, guiding and protecting me.

I ask that if anyone is being abusing in any kind of fashion, *please* get out and get help. Do not stay silent. Go to the police, a friend, a church, a hospital, a shelter, any place where you can be safe. The national hotline number is 1-800-799-7233. You are valuable, and you deserve the life God meant for you. You are precious, and you are loved. Please remember it doesn't start out physical in most cases. It is a process that leads up to it. Don't ignore the red flags. I ask in the name of Jesus that anyone that is reading my book and is being hurt or has a drinking problem or drug problem be covered with the blood of Jesus and find the strength and will power to get help, then to heal. "He heals the brokenhearted and binds up their wounds" (Psalm 147:3). *Love doesn't hurt!*

These are some extra verses you can got to:

Grace

> For by grace you have been saved through faith, and not of yourselves; it is the gift of God. (Ephesians 2:8)

You may also want to read the whole chapter.

> By the grace of God I am what I am, and his grace toward me was not in vain; but I labored more abundantly. (1 Corinthians 15:10)

> The God of all grace, who called us to his eternal glory by Christ Jesus, after you have suffered a while. Perfect, establish, strengthen and settle you. To him be the glory and the dominion forever and ever Amen. (1 Peter 5:10)

His image

Casting down arguments and every high thing that exalts itself against the knowledge of God, bringing every thought into captivity to the obedience of Christ, and being ready to punish all disobedience when your obedience is fulfilled. (2 Corinthians 10:5–6)

So God created man in his own image; in the image of God, He created him; both male and female. (Genesis 1:27)

Forgiveness

Beloved, do not avenge yourselves; but rather give place to wrath; for it is written, Vengeance is mine, I will repay, says the Lord. (Romans 12:19)

Forgive us our debts as we forgive our debtors. (Matthew 6:12)

Judge not, and you shall not be judged. Condemn not, and you shall not be condemned. Forgive, and you will be forgiven. (Luke 6:37)

To forgive to pardon to show mercy.

Protection

He shall cover you with his feathers, and under his wings you shall take refuge; His truth shall be your shield and buckler. (Psalms 91:4)

Please read this whole chapter as it is very powerful. When I pray and cover my home and family, I say I lay Psalm 91 down at the foot of my door to cover my household.

> You will keep him in perfect peace, whose mind is stayed on you, because he trusts in you. (Isaiah 26:3)

> God is in the midst of her, she shall not be moved; God shall help her, just at the break of dawn. (Psalm 45:5)

Anxious: To be afraid of, to be anxious.

> Yea, though I walk through the valley of death I will fear no evil; For you are with me; your rod and your staff, they comfort me. (Psalms 23:4)

> The Lord is my light and my strength; whom shall, I fear? The Lord is the strength of my life; Of whom shall I be afraid? (Psalm 27:1)

> Fear not, for I am with you; Be not dismayed, for I am your God. I will strengthen you, yes, I will help you, I will uphold you with my righteous right hand. (Isaiah 41:10)

God's promise

> I will never leave you nor forsake you. (Hebrews 13:5)

Salvation

> For God so loved the world that he gave his only begotten son that who shall ever believe

in him shall not perish but have ever lasting life.
(John 3:16)

If you do not have Jesus as your Lord and Savior, I urge you to pray this simple prayer:

> Heavenly Father, I believe in you, and I believe you died on the cross and rose from the grave so I might have eternal life. Lord, I want to spend eternity with you. I ask that you come in my heart that I may not perish and that I have everlasting life. Forgive me of my sins. Thank you, Father, that I am born again, and all things are new. Amen.

If you prayed this prayer, welcome to the family. I pray that you heal and that you move forward with the awesome life God has waiting for you and thank you for taking the time out to read my testimony. God bless!

ABOUT THE AUTHOR

Lynn is a mother of two and a grandma of two. Lynn is a CNA in a rehab and nursing center. Lynn's passion is taking care of those who need help. Lynn has been studying to get her certificate in women's ministry and for a license to marry people, which Lynn can proudly say she just received. She is now studying to get her bachelor's degree in chaplaincy for hospice or wherever God takes her with it. Lynn's walk with God is so important to her. God saved her from herself and from others that were trying to destroy her. Lynn thanks God for a praying mother, and she is looking forward to the future that God has in store for her. Lynn knows what it is to have regrets and to want to undo the past. She can't, so she is embracing it and handing it over to the Lord, and she is letting him show her how to help others. Hopefully she will be writing another book. That is her goal, God willing.